Leaders of Religion

THE BUDDHA

Dilwyn Hunt M.A.

OLIVER & BOYD

Acknowledgements

The publishers thank the following for their permission to reproduce photographs on the pages listed:

Camera Press/Sarah Webb Barrell (p. 4) Animal Aid Society Ltd (p. 23) The Buddhist Society (pp. 24, 35, 46) Martin Carter (p. 27) The Mansell Collection (p. 31) Japan Information Centre (p. 47) Ceylon Tourist Board (inside back cover)

The poster on p. 6 is reproduced by kind permission of Argus Communications Ltd, DLM House, Edinburgh Way, Harlow, Essex and is part of an extensive range, featured in their free catalogue, available upon request to Argus.

Illustrated by Joanna Troughton

Oliver & Boyd,
Robert Stevenson House,
1–3 Baxter's Place,
Leith Walk,
Edinburgh EH1 3BB.

A Division of Longman Group UK Limited

First published 1987

Set in 12/14pt Palatino Roman

Produced by Longman Group (FE) Ltd
Printed in Hong Kong

CONTENTS

INTRODUCTION

In a number of world religions certain people are regarded as the great leaders or teachers of that religion. Some of these teachers are called Founders because it was largely through their efforts that a new religion began. Jesus of Nazareth, for example, is often called the Founder of Christianity. Guru Nanak is often called the Founder of Sikhism.

In Buddhism there is one person whose life and teaching helps people to understand more about life. Buddhists believe he was the wisest teacher of all. His name was Siddhartha Gautama but he is known by his special title, the Buddha.

This book looks at the story of the Buddha. Although many people would call the Buddha one of the great leaders of religion, not everyone would agree. Some would say that what the Buddha taught was not really a religion. Unlike other religious leaders, the Buddha did not claim that his ideas came from God. He did not say that people should worship God. In fact there are many Buddhists today who do not believe in a God. Can a person have a religion but not believe in a God? To many people this idea seems very strange.

"What is the purpose of my life?"
"Why do we suffer?"
"What is death?"
"How can I really be happy?"

'"He insulted me, he hurt me, he defeated me, he robbed me." Those who think such thoughts will not be free from hate.'
(The Dhammapada, 1:4)

One thing, however, is certain. The Buddha's teachings do help people to find answers to questions which other world religions like Islam and Christianity also try to answer. These are questions such as: "What is the purpose of my life?" "Why do we suffer?" "What is death?" and "How can I really be happy?"

In this book there are a number of plays, newspaper articles and radio programmes. These are of course imaginary. Even the plays should not be considered as attempts to reconstruct historical events exactly. Their purpose is to introduce readers in a lively and appealing way to one of the greatest men who has ever lived, Gautama the Buddha.

Alongside many of the drawings in this book there are passages taken from the Dhammapada. The Dhammapada is one of the most famous and most popular of all Buddhist scriptures.

A Life of Luxury

We live in a world of advertisements. Every day we are being persuaded to buy more and more things: microwave ovens, cars, smart clothes, beautiful furniture, stereo recorders, video machines and cameras. Every day we are urged to spend more and more money. If we believed the advertisements, money and the things it can buy would be the most important reason for living.

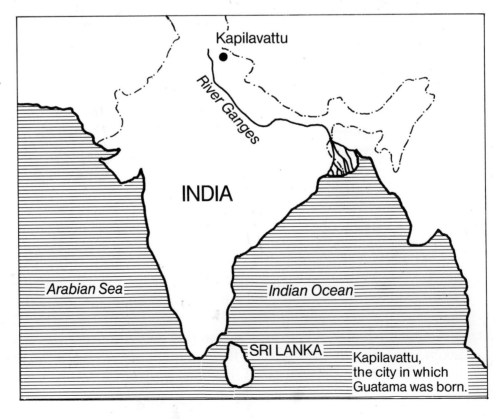

Kapilavattu, the city in which Guatama was born.

'The sensuous pleasures of life flow everywhere. Bound for pleasures and seeking pleasures we suffer life and old age.'

(The Dhammapada, 24:341)

Many people would think that anyone who deliberately gave up a fortune to live a life of poverty was simply stupid. Only a mad person or a fool would do such a thing. Nevertheless, a sane and highly intelligent man did just that. That man's name was called Siddhartha Gautama. He was the man who came to be called the Buddha.

Gautama was born in northern India in the city of Kapilavattu. The date was about 563 BCE. Gautama's father was the leading citizen of Kapilavattu. He was the local ruler. Gautama was a member of one of the noblest and most distinguished families in the region. The family was also very rich, and the young Gautama enjoyed all the things that money could buy. While others lived in misery and poverty, for Gautama there were the pleasures of a luxurious home, magnificent banquets and fine clothes.

'In days gone by this mind of mine used to stray wherever selfish desire or lust or pleasure would lead it. Today this mind does not stray and is under the harmony of control, even as a wild elephant is controlled by the trainer.'

(The Dhammapada, 23:326)

Gautama married a woman called Yasodhara. She too was the daughter of noble and wealthy parents. Gautama and Yasodhara lived happily together and this happiness increased when Yasodhara gave birth to a baby boy. Gautama seemed to have everything he could possibly wish for.

Yet Gautama felt that something was missing from his life. He became aware that whether one was poor or rich, life was never perfect. Certain questions began to trouble his mind: "Why is life full of disappointments?" "Why do we suffer?" "What is life?" Gautama felt an urgent need to find the answers to these questions. However, in spite of all his wealth, he could not buy the answers.

For Gautama the questions about pain and suffering, life and death had to be answered. He believed that it was only by answering them that real happiness could be found. He decided that he would have to search for the answers himself. Perhaps the answers were to be found by living with the sadhu, the holy men of the forest?

Late one night Gautama gently entered Yasodhara's bedroom. He looked lovingly on her and his child as they slept. Then silently, with a heavy but determined heart, he rode away from his life of luxury. Gautama had given up everything to search for Truth. He was twenty-nine years old.

'A person may find pain in doing good as long as that good has not given fruit; but when the fruit of good comes then that person finds good indeed.'

(The Dhammapada, 9:120)

The Beginning of the Journey

Cast: Gautama
Channa: Gautama's servant and charioteer

Scene: It is the dead of night and Gautama is trying to wake up his
loyal servant, Channa.

GAUTAMA: Wake up, Channa! Wake up!

CHANNA: My Lord! What is it? Is there something wrong?
(*Charioteer*)

GAUTAMA: Get dressed, Channa. I need you. You are to saddle two of my horses
and ride with me.

CHANNA: What are you doing? Where are we going?

GAUTAMA: I am leaving, Channa, now. I am going to live with the sadhu, the
holy men who live in the forest.

CHANNA: My Lord you cannot! You are a wealthy man. To live with the sadhu
you must become penniless.

GAUTAMA: I know, Channa. Today I am giving up everything forever. My
wealth, my jewels, everything I have I abandon.

CHANNA: I cannot believe it. You have everything a person could want. The sadhu sleep on the ground with only the trees to protect them.

GAUTAMA: I know. They dress in only a simple cloth and eat only crumbs.

CHANNA: I beg you, Lord, don't go. Such a life would kill you.

GAUTAMA: Channa, every night of my life I have slept in a warm bed. Every day I have worn the finest clothes, eaten the best food. Yet my life of luxury has not brought me happiness.

CHANNA: I do not understand. You have had everything in life, horses to ride, games to play, servants...

GAUTAMA: Pleasures, Channa. My life has been full of pleasures. Yet I know that in my life there is something missing. In all this luxury I cannot find real happiness. Perhaps I can find it amongst the holy men of the forest.

CHANNA: Your wife, Lord Gautama. What of your wife and child?

GAUTAMA: My heart breaks to leave them but leave them I must. So far in life I have had everything, now I must learn to live with nothing. Come! Tonight I begin my journey in search of the Truth.

**'It is you who must make the effort.
The Great of the past
only showed the way.'**
(The Dhammapada, 20:276)

10

What have you remembered?

True or False   Which box has the true answer in it?

1. Siddhartha Gautama was born in the country of

India	China

2. Siddhartha Gautama lived over 500 years

before Jesus of Nazareth	after Jesus of Nazareth

3. Followers of the Buddha are called

Buddhists	Indians

4. As a young man Gautama was

very wealthy	very poor

5. As a young man Gautama became aware that money

did not bring real happiness	was the secret of real happiness

6. At the age of twenty-nine Gautama

married and enjoyed a life of luxury	left his wealth and family

7. Gautama felt that when he had everything life was

still often empty and unsatisfying	always perfect and full of lasting pleasures

8. Later in his life Siddhartha Gautama was given the title

the Prophet	the Buddha

What do you know?

9. Name three countries which today have a large Buddhist population.
10. Name two great religions, apart from Buddhism, which began in India.
11. Why do some people say that Buddhism is not really a religion?
12. Why do some people say that Buddhism is a religion?

What do you think?

13. Imagine you are Gautama's charioteer, Channa. You have returned to Kapilavattu after saying goodbye to Gautama. Yasodhara, Gautama's wife, has sent for you. What do you think Channa and Yasodhara would have said to each other?
14. Look at the cartoon drawing on page 6. What do you think the cartoon is telling us?
15. Some people could be described as being materialistic. What does being 'materialistic' mean?

UNIT 2

The Great Awakening

Alone, penniless and dressed in no more than a simple cloth, Gautama began his great search for Truth. Gautama was convinced that there was a way for everyone to be really happy and content. He was sure that in spite of sickness and death, people could find real happiness. Yet Gautama also believed that no one could find happiness unless they understood why suffering was a part of everyone's life. Nor could anyone find happiness unless they faced the truth that one day they would die.

He visited holy men and listened to what they had to say. From them he learned many things. But no one gave him the answers that would satisfy him.

One day in the forest he met five men who like himself were puzzled by the questions of life and death, happiness and suffering. They joined Gautama and they agreed to work together in order to discover the mystery of life itself. They made a rule for themselves about how they would live. Through hardship and discipline they would find the secret of true happiness. They believed, perhaps, that if they ignored their bodies, their spirits would become stronger. In this way they thought that they would find the key to happiness.

'If on the journey of life
anyone can find a wise and
intelligent friend who is
good and self-controlled,
let them go with that traveller;
and in joy and recollection
let them overcome the dangers
of the journey.'
(The Dhammapada, 23:328)

'Neither nakedness, nor entangled hair, nor uncleanliness, nor fasting, nor sleeping on the ground, nor covering the body with ashes, nor ever-squatting, can purify anyone who is not pure from doubts and desires.'
(The Dhammapada, 10:141)

'The gift of Truth conquers all gifts. The taste of Truth conquers all sweetness. The Joy of Truth conquers all pleasures. The loss of desires conquers all sorrows.'
(The Dhammapada, 24:354)

Gautama was very determined. He starved himself until his body became skin and bones. He spent long hours training himself to sit still. He shivered in the cold of the night. He suffered in the heat of the day.

Yet, in spite of all his efforts, Gautama could not find the answers to the questions which still troubled him. At last he realised that these answers, the true Enlightenment he sought, could not be found by punishing himself in this way. For six long years Gautama and his five friends had been together, but now they parted.

Alone again, Gautama sat down under the branches of a tree. He began to think about all the things in his life he had seen and learned. His mind pondered deeper and deeper. Hour after hour passed. Suddenly, like a brilliant light at the end of a long tunnel, the answer to the mystery of life itself flashed before him. At last he knew his search was over. He sat motionless. He was perfectly happy. It was like waking up. Now he had an understanding of life. He had found Enlightenment. Gautama was now the Buddha, the Enlightened One.

The Great Awakening

Cast: Kondanna: A follower of the Buddha
       Samala: A non-Buddhist. The wife of Kuta
       Kuta: A non-Buddhist. The husband of Samala

Scene: Kondanna meets two people who have heard rumours of the
       Buddha. He explains to them about the Buddha's
       Enlightenment.

SAMALA: What rubbish! You mean to say that this man sat under a tree for a couple of hours and now you call him the Buddha!

KUTA: What does it mean anyway? The Buddha . . . it must mean something.

KONDANNA: It is a title. The Buddha means the Enlightened One.

SAMALA: So it's not his real name?

KONDANNA: Not really. When he was born he was given the name Siddhartha Gautama, but we never call him that. He is always known to us as the Buddha.

KUTA: Gautama . . . isn't he the man who suddenly disappeared? The one who left his wife and child and a huge fortune?

SAMALA: I remember. And this is the man who you say is the Buddha, the Enlightened One? You must be mad!

KONDANNA: Mad . . . perhaps. Yet amazing things do happen all around us. I believe a caterpillar can one day become a butterfly. I believe an acorn could one day become an oak. I believe someone can search for Truth and find it. Is that so mad?

SAMALA: All right then. You say Gautama suddenly became the Buddha about a year ago?

KONDANNA: That's right.

KUTA: So, what happened? Did God speak to him or something?

KONDANNA: No, it wasn't like that. The Buddha's Enlightenment did not come from God.

SAMALA: Well, where did it come from?

KONDANNA: Enlightenment comes from yourself. The Buddha found Enlightenment for himself.

KUTA: Not from the gods?

KONDANNA: No, Enlightenment came to Gautama through his own efforts. He wanted to understand the truth about life and death, so he thought hard about it. He did that himself, it was not God.

SAMALA:	I'm not understanding anything. Enlightenment . . . life and death . . . what does all that mean?
KONDANNA:	Perhaps the Buddha's Enlightenment was like waking up. Until the Buddha's Enlightenment, every one of us was in some way asleep.
SAMALA:	(*Yawn!*) I'm beginning to nod off myself.
KONDANNA:	Samala, when you sleep do you have dreams?
SAMALA:	Of course I have dreams. Everyone has dreams.
KUTA:	Sometimes I dream I can fly. Once I remember dreaming that I had won the great archery contest in Savatthi.
KONDANNA:	When you woke up, were you disappointed that you couldn't fly or that you hadn't won the archery contest?
SAMALA:	Of course he wasn't. Dreams don't really matter do they? Not when you wake up.
KONDANNA:	Exactly! Becoming Enlightened like the Buddha *is* like waking up. The things which you thought were so important . . . money, fame, popularity, power . . . suddenly you see that these things don't really matter at all.
KUTA:	So you mean becoming Enlightened isn't really like learning lots of new things? It's more like seeing the world differently?
KONDANNA:	That's right. It's seeing the world *truly*. It's waking up and seeing the world as it really is.
SAMALA:	Hold it! Are you saying that when the Buddha became Enlightened things like . . . money, fame, power . . . just didn't matter to him any more. Can all of us become Enlightened—not just the Buddha?
KONDANNA:	That's right. What's more it is only when you stop wanting all those things that you will find real happiness. To want those things makes you a prisoner. You are caught in a trap.
KUTA:	Enlightenment brings freedom from wanting, freedom from desire. With this freedom you will at last find joy.
KONDANNA:	Yes. Desire is the cause of human unhappiness. You must come and hear the Buddha explain it all himself. You too might find Enlightenment.
KUTA:	I might just do that. What about you Samala?
SAMALA:	I'm thinking . . .

What have you remembered?

1. Gautama left his home to find:

a huge sum of money	**a second beautiful wife**
a land in which he could be king	**an answer to how everyone could be really happy**

2. In the forest Gautama, along with five other men, agreed to:

indulge themselves in every possible pleasure	**live without the usual pleasures of life**
build a temple in which they worshipped the gods	**cut down trees and sell wood**

3. When Gautama lived in the forest he:

ate normally	**ate only meat**
starved himself	**ate everything he could find**

4. When Gautama achieved Enlightenment:

he believed he had found perfect happiness	**he believed God gave him certain laws**
he felt unhappy and sad	**he believed he had had some sort of dream**

5. At the moment Gautama achieved Enlightenment he:

believed a holy man appeared and spoke to him	**understood life as it really is**
decided to go back to his family	**believed that God gave him a holy book**

6. Gautama believed that:

he was the only person who could find Enlightenment	**no one could find Enlightenment**

only by punishing himself could he find Enlightenment	everyone could find Enlightenment

7. Some followers of the Buddha describe Gautama's Enlightenment as:

the great Awakening	the great Dream
the great Sleep	the great Hardship

8. The Buddha taught that people would find perfect happiness only when:

they had lots of money or fame	they lived on their own in a forest and starved
having money or fame was no longer important to them	they believed in and accepted the will of God

What do you know?

9. For how many years did Gautama punish himself?

10. What does the title 'the Buddha' mean?

11. When Buddhists refer to Gautama's Enlightenment what event are they talking about?

12. The Buddha gave up a life of luxury. He also gave up a life of great hardship. He began a new way of life. What is the name Buddhists give to this new way of life?

What do you think?

13. Why do you think that Gautama felt that he had to give up all of his wealth and leave his family?

14. Gautama wanted to find an answer to 'the mystery of life itself'. What do you think this means?

15. Gautama's 'Enlightenment' changed his life and the way he thought about everything. Many people, including other great leaders of religion, say that something has happened to them which suddenly changed their lives. Can you think of any examples?

16. In what way, if any, was Gautama's 'Enlightenment' special or different from what happened to other leaders of religion?

The Wandering Sage

After his Enlightenment the Buddha, as he was now called, began teaching others. Many of the people who listened to him found that by following what he said, they found a new kind of peace in their lives.

In the first year of his Enlightenment the Buddha visited his family in Kapilavattu. He helped them to understand why he had left. Some members of his family later accepted his teaching and became his followers.

As the Buddha travelled around, even rich and famous people listened to his teaching. He told one king, King Pasendi, that a king should use power to help other people, not to trample on them. He once said, "If the king mercilessly plunders his people, how can he expect them not to steal from each other?" Another king, called Bimbisara, became a good friend and supporter of the Buddha.

'Look upon the person who tells you your faults as if they had told you of a hidden treasure.'
(The Dhammapada, 6:76)

Some of the people who listened to the Buddha left their homes and travelled with him. These followers were known as the Sangha. The Buddha spent many hours with the Sangha helping them to achieve Enlightenment. However, the Sangha did not stay with the Buddha all the time. They would go out on their own to explain the Buddha's teaching in the villages and towns they visited.

During the rainy season of June, July and August, when it was not possible to travel, the Buddha stayed at a vihara. A vihara was a special building in which members of the Sangha lived. They were usually in quiet groves or gardens just outside large cities. The Buddha established many viharas.

'Wealth destroys the fool
who seeks not the Beyond.
Because of greed for wealth
the fool destroys himself
as if he were his own enemy.'
(The Dhammapada, 24:335)

Today Buddhist viharas are to be found all over the world. The men and women who live in them follow a way of life which is very like the way the first Sangha lived. All members of the Sangha, today as in the past, accept five basic rules:

1. **Not to cause an injury to any living thing**
2. **Not to take anything which has not been given freely**
3. **Not to be involved in sexual immorality**
4. **Not to lie**
5. **Not to take alcohol or drugs**

Himalayan HERALD

ISSUE 2877   18K

THE VOICE OF THE NATION

BUDDHA LETS IN WOMEN

Gautama. The so-called Buddha

The so-called Buddha said yesterday that women can now be members of his Sangha. He also said that women may live in any one of the many viharas which are now to be found all over the country.

ENLIGHTENED
The Buddha has made it clear that women as well as men can benefit from his teaching. He also said that both women and men can become Enlightened.

FIVE HUNDRED
Already over five hundred women have joined his Sangha including Prajapati, the Buddha's own aunt, and Yasodhara, the woman he married before his Enlightenment.

PROTEST
The Buddha's announcement is certain to spark off a storm of protest. Few people accept that women have equality with men, particularly in religious matters.

SUPPORT
However, followers of the Buddha were last night supporting his decision. Rosala, one of the women who joined the Sangha, said, "What a brave step the Buddha has taken by allowing women into the Sangha. Women have been treated for too long by men as if they were servants. The Buddha is prepared to acknowledge women as people. He says that women as well as men have a right to seek the holy life, if that is what they wish."

ANANDA
The Buddha's loyal friend, Ananda, has also backed the Buddha's decision. In fact, Ananda played an important part in persuading the Buddha to accept women into the Sangha.

(FULL STORY See centre pages)

Prajapati and Yasodhara have joined the Sangha

20

SPECIAL REPORT
THE BUDDHA'S SANGHA

The Buddha's Sangha has grown rapidly in just a few years. This is remarkable especially when one thinks of the vows which all members of the Sangha make.

VOWS

The Sangha members all promise to give up seeking wealth and to live a life of poverty. They own nothing except a robe and a bowl for their food. They also make a vow promising not to harm anything and that includes animals! Lying is forbidden and so also are alcohol and drugs. Drink and drugs are said to interfere with the mind and so prevent Enlightenment. Sex is also forbidden to members of the Sangha. In fact sexual attraction for many seems simply to be a desire they have overcome.

ADMIRED

In many towns and cities Buddhists are deeply admired. Some people think they are holy people. So high is the reputation of the Sangha that many people believe it is a privilege to give them food. This is in fact how the Sangha survive. Members humbly accept whatever is given to them. Even if they are given only a few scraps of food they are never disappointed or angry. Their calm and dignified behaviour at all times is very impressive.

HAPPY

Happiness is also an obvious feature of the Sangha. King Pasendi himself has said that the Buddha and his followers seem to be always happy and free from worry. Describing the Buddha's followers he said that they "seem to enjoy life. They have happy smiles like healthy children."

A member of the Sangha

What have you remembered?

Complete the sentences.   Match the phrases in the left-hand column with the words from the right.

1.	The king who became a supporter of the Buddha was called	viharas
2.	The community of followers who formed themselves around the Buddha were called the	food
3.	Members of the Sangha travelled around and explained the teaching of the	Bimbisara
4.	The special buildings in which the Buddha and his followers sometimes lived were called	Sangha
5.	The reputation of the Sangha is so high that many people believe it is a privilege to give them	Buddha

True or False   Which box has the true answer in it?

6. After his Enlightenment the Buddha:

decided to keep what he knew to himself	decided to teach what he knew to others

7. When the Buddha taught:

even the rich and famous took notice	the rich and famous laughed at him and sent him away

8. The Buddha believed that he and his followers should:

keep well away from people and stay in monasteries	live close to cities and towns and talk to people

9. King Pasendi said that the followers of the Buddha looked:

thin, pale and haggard	happy and free from worry

10. When he talked to kings and rulers the Buddha:

was careful not to say anything that would annoy them	told them if he thought that they were wrong

What do you know?

11. Many people were shocked when the Buddha allowed women into the Sangha. Why were they shocked?

12. Why do Buddhists believe that it is wrong to take drink or drugs?

13. Describe some of the ways in which people changed when they became followers of the Buddha.

14. Every member of a Buddhist Sangha accepts five basic rules. What are those rules?

15. Is there a Buddhist Vihara or a Buddhist Society near where you live? Try to find out the address of your nearest Buddhist Vihara or Buddhist Society. Write to them and ask them for information about their organisation.

What do you think?

16. The Dhammapada is one of the most famous and most popular of all Buddhist scriptures. Choose either the passage from the Dhammapada on page 18 'Look upon the person who tells you your faults . . .' or the passage on page 19 'Wealth destroys the fool . . .' and write a story about what you think the passage means.

17. This photograph shows a rabbit being used to test a new cosmetic. The rabbit may not be killed but it may suffer great pain or even blindness. What do you think of experiments of this kind?

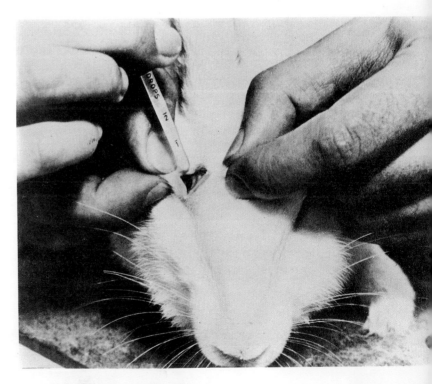

18. Try to get in touch with Buddhists near where you live. Find out what they think of experiments of this kind.

UNIT 4

You are Buddha

'It is easy to see the faults of others, but difficult to see one's own faults. One shows the faults of others like chaff winnowed in the wind, but one conceals one's own faults as a cunning gambler conceals his dice.'
(The Dhammapada, 18:252)

As time went on the Buddha's reputation grew. He often sat in the shade of a tree talking, listening and answering questions. As he and his followers had taken a vow of poverty they each wore only a simple yellow robe and they each ate only one small meal a day. The Buddha's day-to-day life was simple, quiet and peaceful. Thousands flocked to hear him teach. They came because he gave people real hope that they could find true happiness.

The Buddha taught that everyone could become a Buddha like himself. Everyone could become Enlightened and so find true peace and joy. Many Buddhists today believe that the purpose of life is for everyone to become a Buddha. "Look within yourself," they might say, "you are Buddha."

Like Gautama, these present-day Buddhists have taken a vow of poverty. They wear only a simple robe and eat only one meal a day.

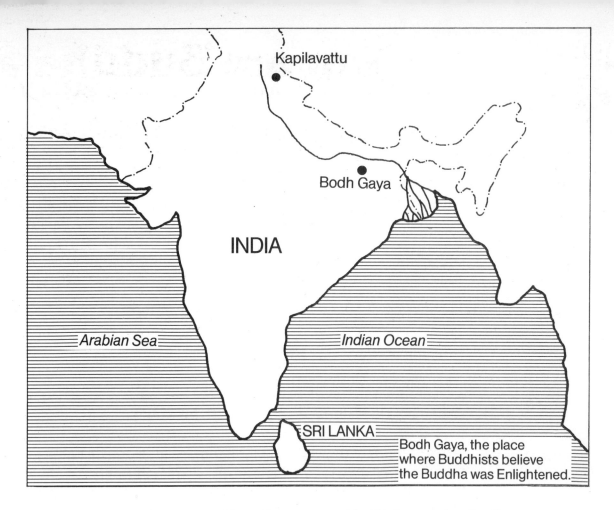

Bodh Gaya, the place where Buddhists believe the Buddha was Enlightened.

When the Buddha was teaching he never said, ''Believe what I tell you and you will be saved.'' He claimed that his teaching was only a guide for people. People should try out his ideas for themselves. He warned that he was not some sort of superhuman saviour. No one could become Enlightened, the Buddha believed, unless they tried for themselves. To find real inner peace, or 'Nirvana', as he called it, you have to rely on yourself. No one can achieve Nirvana for you.

The Buddha never found fault with other people's beliefs. He would never debate with people in order to put them down or to make himself appear clever. He believed that each person had to find her or his own way to Enlightenment. This might take many years or even many lifetimes. In time, he believed, every person could find Enlightenment. Enlightenment would come when people at last understood what the Buddha called the Four Noble Truths.

THE FOUR NOBLE TRUTHS

1. All is dissatisfaction or suffering

2. The cause of all dissatisfaction is desire

3. The cure of all dissatisfaction is to rid oneself of desire

4. The way to rid oneself of desire is by following the Eightfold Path

---

The Four Noble Truths
The Magadha Broadcasting Company (MBC)

Cast: Gautama: the Buddha
Nema: MBC Interviewer
Kamala: MBC Interviewer/Presenter

KAMALA:
(*Presenter*)
Welcome to 'Religion Alive'. The question we are dealing with tonight is, "What does the Buddha teach?" To help us to find some answers we have with us in the studio the Buddha himself, Siddhartha Gautama.

(*The Buddha silently nods and smiles.*)

KAMALA: (*Turning to the Buddha.*) Lord Buddha, an important part of your teaching is what you call 'the Four Noble Truths'.

THE BUDDHA: Yes. The first truth is 'All is suffering'.

NEMA:
(*Interviewer*)
What does that mean? It sounds very miserable.

THE BUDDHA: 'All is suffering' does not mean that life is always sad. It means that always one feels discontented or dissatisfied with life.

KAMALA: Discontented with life! But that's just nonsense isn't it? How can one feel discontented with life when there are so many things which give pleasure?

THE BUDDHA: That's true. There are many pleasures to be enjoyed—food, drink, fun and laughter. But ask yourself honestly, do any of these things give happiness for long? Do they ever really satisfy? You can fill youself with delicious food and wear diamonds on every finger but they will not bring you lasting happiness.

NEMA: So you believe that even people who have money still feel discontented with life?

THE BUDDHA: Yes, very much so.

KAMALA: Do you really believe that?

THE BUDDHA: I know this to be true. Once I had money, a fortune in fact. I know money can bring a kind of happiness. It can make life comfortable. But I also know that money can never bring what I call real happiness.

NEMA: So even the rich feel discontent?

THE BUDDHA: But of course. Some of the wealthiest people in the world feel that life is empty and worthless. When they have everything they still feel that they want something more.

KAMALA: But let's be realistic, money *can* make life better. Surely a person who lives in a small hut would be happier in a big house?

THE BUDDHA:	Would they? In a way perhaps, but a big house would not make that person happy for long. Such things do not give lasting happiness.
NEMA:	You think they would soon desire more?
THE BUDDHA:	Of course. You see when we have things we soon take them for granted. Something which once gave us great pleasure—after a while it seems dull.
NEMA:	For many people even a cheap bottle of wine is a treat but it would not satisfy a rich person. Those people who can afford wine every day take even expensive wine for granted.
THE BUDDHA:	That's right. Perfect and lasting happiness does not come by having more and more things. It comes to those people who can be happy within themselves. This is why there is discontent with life. All is suffering because few have learnt to be content within themselves.
KAMALA:	Well, so much for the first of your Noble Truths. We will take a short break there. Join us again after the news headlines.

What is really for sale in this shop? Can you really buy satisfaction?
Can money buy happiness?

KAMALA: Welcome back to part two. In the first part of our programme we discussed the Buddha's first Noble Truth, 'All is suffering'. The second of the Buddha's Noble Truths is, 'Desire is the cause of all suffering'.

THE BUDDHA: Yes, it is desire which robs people of perfect happiness. A bigger house, nicer clothes, a softer bed, a better job, a different lover, even if satisfied such desires do not bring contentment.

NEMA: That's all very well but what about friendship, love and family? Can't we find real contentment in the enjoyment of these things?

THE BUDDHA: Lasting happiness is not found even in the love and comfort of your own family. Death takes away everything, even those we love. In everything there is suffering and discontent.

NEMA: Yet you claim that there is a cure for this suffering?

THE BUDDHA: Yes, the cure for suffering is to rid yourself of desire. This is the third Noble Truth.

KAMALA: Well, how can you do that? How can you rid yourself of desire?

THE BUDDHA: Only slowly and with much effort. Like a warrior who trains to conquer an enemy, so you must train yourself. You must conquer within yourself the enemies of hate, greed and pride.

NEMA: Is this what you call the Eightfold Path?

THE BUDDHA: Yes. The Eightfold Path is the way by which you learn. You learn to control your body, control your words, control your mind and control your whole inner self.

NEMA: The Eightfold Path I should point out is the fourth of the Noble Truths.

THE BUDDHA: That's correct. It is the path that leads to total self-control, perfect happiness, or what we call Nirvana.

KAMALA: And by following this Eightfold Path you claim it is possible to remove all desires?

THE BUDDHA: Not many people do achieve this, I admit, but it is possible. Those who can rid themselves of desire will find Nirvana.

KAMALA: Well thank you, Lord Buddha. (*Turning to audience.*) We shall be looking in more detail at the Eightfold Path in our programme next week. Join us then.

What have you remembered?

1. Complete the word puzzle.

Clues across

1. The Buddha said that everyone had to find his or her own way to this.
4. Before he achieved Enlightenment the Buddha was called this.
6. The Buddha said that there were four of these.
8. An inner enemy which one had to conquer.
9. The Buddha said that everyone could become this.
10. One of the rules of the Sangha means that you shouldn't do this.
11. The cause of all suffering.
12. The Buddha said that his teaching was only this.

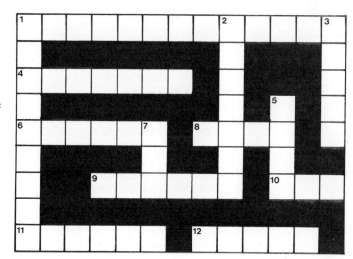

Clues down

1. The path which led to Nirvana.
2. The end of all desire, perfect bliss.
3. Thousands of people came to hear the Buddha do this.
5. The Buddha and his followers had only one of these each day.
7. All is dissatisfaction but life is not always this.

What do you know?

2. What was the fourth of the Buddha's Noble Truths?
3. When the Buddha talked about desires what sort of things did he have in mind?

What do you think?

4. Some people fill in the football pools in the hope of winning a large sum of money. Do you think having money always brings happiness?
5. From magazines and newspapers make a collection of advertisements which try to increase people's desire to have things. What do you think the Buddha would have said about such advertisements?
6. What do you think are the dangers of advertising?
7. What do you think is the value of advertising?
8. What do you think it was about the Buddha that made his teaching attractive?

The Serene Mind

One day a man went to the Buddha and insulted him. The Buddha remained silent and calm. When the man stopped speaking the Buddha said, "Listen carefully, if a person does me wrong I will return to that person only my love. The more evil that comes from a person, the more goodness shall come from me." The man, although startled by this reply, only insulted the Buddha more. The Buddha smiled at him and said, "My son, a person who insults another is like one who throws mud into the air. The mud does not spoil the air, it only falls back and spoils the thrower." The man went away ashamed. Later he returned to become a follower of the Buddha.

No matter what happened the Buddha was always perfectly calm. His mind was untroubled. He was always serene. Even when he met a fierce robber called Angulimala the Buddha did not worry. The Buddha's serenity persuaded Angulimala to turn away from a life of crime and violence.

How did the Buddha achieve such inner serenity towards all things and all people? The Buddha did not believe that he or anyone could achieve perfect peace in one lifetime. He believed that all people would be reborn after they died. It was only after many rebirths that a person would at last achieve Nirvana. The Buddha taught that slowly a person's heart became more compassionate, and their mind became more serene. Only when that person had achieved Nirvana would she or he be freed from the cycle of birth, death and rebirth.

'Overcome anger by peacefulness;
overcome evil by good.
Overcome the mean by generosity;
and the man who lies by truth.'
(The Dhammapada, 17:223)

The Tibetan man is holding a prayer wheel. The wheel in Buddhism is a symbol of rebirth. A wheel cannot go forward without turning round. Buddhists believe that no person can move closer towards Nirvana without being reborn many times.

The Buddha taught that it was the Eightfold Path which led to Nirvana. The Eightfold Path is set out below. Buddhists usually group the Path into three parts: Wisdom, Morality and Meditation.

THE EIGHTFOLD PATH
1. Right Understanding 2. Right Thought   ]—WISDOM
3. Right Speech 4. Right Action 5. Right Occupation   ]—MORALITY
6. Right Effort 7. Right Mindfulness 8. Right Concentration   ]—MEDITATION

The Buddha said that it was not necessary to start with the first on the list, Right Understanding, then pass on to number two and so on in order through the Eightfold Path. Progress in any one part of the Path comes when one also tries to make progress in the other parts as well. Each part of the Path ties up with the other parts.

Right Speech meant not lying but it also meant being careful not to hurt others when speaking. Words should always be courteous and true.

Right Action meant not doing anything which harmed another living creature but it also meant accepting the five rules of the Sangha (page 19).

Right Occupation meant that work (or occupation) must not depend on being discourteous, untrue or harmful to others. It meant that daily work should not conflict with any other part of the Path.

The Buddha believed that Right Speech, Right Action and Right Occupation were very important. He also believed that progress towards Nirvana would not be made by good actions alone. One also needed to practise Meditation. Meditation helps people to remain calm no matter what happens. Right Effort, Right Mindfulness and Right Concentration help people to become more open and more aware. They show that greed, envy and anger need have no place in one's life. Instead, through meditation compassionate and just thoughts will be encouraged.

Wisdom comes from having a Right Understanding of the Buddha's teaching. It also comes from understanding the right reason for everything that a person does.

The Buddha showed that by following the Eightfold Path people could rid themselves of desire. They could achieve that inner state of serenity which he called Nirvana.

Tanzan and Ekido

Here is a famous story first told by Japanese Buddhist teachers. Tanzan and Ekido are two Buddhist monks. Only one of them has properly learnt from the Buddha's teaching. Which monk is it?

TANZAN AND EKIDO WERE ONCE TRAVELLING TOGETHER.

COMING AROUND A BEND THEY MET A WOMAN WHO COULD NOT CROSS THE RIVER.

TANZAN WADED ACROSS THE RIVER...

...AND CARRIED THE WOMAN TO THE OTHER BANK.

THE WOMAN THANKED TANZAN AND EKIDO AND SAID FAREWELL.

THE TWO MEN CONTINUED THEIR JOURNEY.

EKIDO DID NOT SPEAK AGAIN FOR SEVERAL HOURS.

WE MONKS DON'T GO NEAR FEMALES, ESPECIALLY NOT YOUNG AND LOVELY ONES. IT IS DANGEROUS, WHY DID YOU DO THAT?

I LEFT THE WOMAN BACK THERE. ARE YOU STILL CARRYING HER?

THEN HE COULD RESTRAIN HIMSELF NO LONGER.

The Mind Aware

Cast: Visakha: A young Buddhist
Pakati: A young Buddhist
Ananda: The Buddha's most faithful follower. He has been
with the Buddha for many years

VISAKHA: Ananda, you are the Buddha's most faithful friend. Will you help us
to understand the words of the Enlightened One?

ANANDA: My young friends, I am but a learner myself, yet I will help you if I
can. What is it you do not understand?

PAKATI: Meditation, Ananda. We do not understand fully what the Buddha
says about meditation.

VISAKHA: What does it mean to 'become mindful', Ananda? How should we
meditate?

ANANDA: There are many others who know more than I do but perhaps I can
help a little. When you meditate, sit perfectly still.

PAKATI: Should we sit cross-legged on the floor, Ananda, or on a chair?

ANANDA: Gentle Pakati, it does not matter. Both are good. When you are
comfortable, think about your breathing. Breathe in and out normally,
but let your mind be totally aware of your breathing. Concentrate
your mind upon your breathing.

VISAKHA: I have tried to do that, Ananda, but my mind wanders.

ANANDA: Then you must try harder, Visakha. Practise every day. You will find
that slowly your mind will become more fully aware of everything
that happens around you.

PAKATI: You mean that we will fall asleep?

ANANDA: It is nothing like sleep, Pakati. You will feel more awake than you
have ever felt in your life. Worries about events in the past or in the
future will not disturb you. Your mind will be full of what is
happening here and now at this very moment. Meditation will help
you to achieve this.

PAKATI: So you mean that whether I am eating, talking, walking or sitting, I should try to be completely aware of what I am doing?

ANANDA: Yes, always live in the present. Do not let anything else distract you. In this way you will experience great calm and tranquillity.

VISAKHA: The calm and tranquillity of Nirvana?

ANANDA: The more you practise meditation the better. You will gain more from it. You will learn to think about things which are good. You will learn not to let anger from the past or desire for the future destroy your peace of mind now, in the present.

PAKATI: Is this true, Ananda? Is such peace, such serenity possible?

ANANDA: My friends, you must not take my word for it. You must try it for yourselves.

Buddhists meditating. Buddhists believe that meditation can help to develop awareness, calmness and tranquillity.

What have you remembered?

1. When insulted the Buddha:

always remained calm	insulted people back
became angry and violent	ordered his followers to defend him

2. Buddhists believe that usually when a person dies they:

automatically achieve Nirvana	will remain dead until a final judgement day
will never live again in any way	are reborn to live again on earth

3. The Buddha encouraged his followers to practise regularly:

starving themselves	telling other people their faults
sitting still in meditation	worshipping the gods

4. Through following the Eightfold Path, Buddhists believe a person can become:

more clever	more greedy
more quarrelsome	more serene

5. When meditating, Buddhists often:

concentrate on God	concentrate on their breathing
concentrate on nothing but let their minds wander	fall asleep

6. Buddhists believe that meditation helps a person to:

become fully aware of the present	be reborn	breathe easily
	have a good rest	

7. Buddhists believe that meditation can prevent a person from:

falling asleep	responding to angry thoughts
being calm	being happy

8. A person who is serene is usually:

angry and irritable	jealous and envious
silent and moody	calm and content

What do you know?

9. What happened when the Buddha was attacked by the fierce robber, Angulimala?

10. What do you think the story of Angulimala tells us about the Buddha?

11. Buddhists believe that when anyone achieves Nirvana that person becomes free. Free from what?

12. Buddhists believe in rebirth. What does rebirth mean?

What do you think?

13. The Buddha believed that people damaged themselves if they had angry thoughts or performed violent actions. What do you think he meant by this? What truth, if any, is there in this claim?

14. Right Occupation is the fifth of the Buddha's Eightfold Path. What do you think the Buddha would have said was a 'right occupation'?

15. What do you think the Buddha would have said was a wrong occupation?

16. Read carefully through the story of Tanzan and Ekido on pages 32–33. What do you think this story is telling us?

17. What do Buddhists believe can be gained from meditation?

Become Selfless

Most people think of themselves first. They are ego-centred. The Buddha believed that putting ourselves before everything or anyone else prevents people from gaining real happiness.

'I', 'me' and 'mine'—so often people use these words. So often people fight and argue—'that's mine', 'that belongs to me', 'this is what I want'. It is this belief in the self, 'I', 'me' and 'mine', which is the cause of so much greed, envy, hatred and violence in the world. It is because people put themselves before everything or anyone else that real care and compassion for others is so rare. We say, "I want to do well at this job", so we become envious when someone else does better. We say, "I want to marry that person", so we become jealous when they marry someone else. We say, "I disagree with you", so we shout and argue. We say, "I have been insulted", so we fight and hurt each other.

Although the Buddha taught that everyone could achieve Nirvana, he believed that very few people would really gain Enlightenment. To live in perfect contentment, a person had to become selfless and let go of all desire. One had to let go of the belief in the self.

The Parable of Me and Mine

The parable or story of Me and Mine was first told by Indian Buddhist teachers.

Two children, Sarida and Nina, were playing on a beach making sandcastles.

When the sandcastles were finished the two children started to argue.

Becoming angry, Nina kicked at Sarida's castle.

Furious, Sarida ruined Nina's castle. The two children started to fight.

Nina made Sarida's nose bleed. Sarida poked Nina in the eye and pulled her hair.

Still angry but now hurt, they stopped fighting and went back to their sandcastles.

When evening came they both thought that they ought to go home.

The sea washed over the two castles but the two children no longer cared. They turned away and went home.

The Buddha said that when anyone achieved Enlightenment that person 'woke up'. She or he realised that thinking of oneself first was not the way to understanding. Only when they at last realised this would they be free from greed, envy and violence. Then they would be filled with compassion and love for all things.

Although the Buddha taught compassion and love, not everyone liked what he said. Some of the religious priests disliked the Buddha. These priests sacrificed animals as part of their religious faith but the Buddha said that such killing was wrong. As we have already learnt, the Buddha allowed women to join the Sangha and this came as a shock to some people who thought that women were of little value, except as servants.

The Buddha also angered some people who believed they were better than others. He gave them no special attention. The Buddha was just as happy to teach a beggar as a king, a criminal as a priest. He ignored people's social position. He even accepted into the Sangha people who were called the 'Outcastes'. This again deeply shocked and angered some people. Outcastes were avoided by many people and were treated as if they were unclean and untouchable.

Some people hated the Buddha because they were jealous of him. The Buddha's own cousin, a man called Devadatta, was so full of hate that he tried to kill the Buddha by arranging for a maddened elephant to attack him.

'O let us live in joy, in love amongst those who hate! Among who hate, let us live in love.'
(The Dhammapada, 15:197)

The Peacemaker

The Koshala Television Association (KTA)

Cast: Madri: Reporter to the KTA
       Nanda: War correspondent to the KTA
       Marada: Lord of the Sakyas
       Vasu: Lord of the Koliyas
       Gautama: The Buddha

MADRI:
(*Reporter*) The tension is unbearable here at Vesali. The Sakyas army and the army of the Koliyas are lined up and it looks as if a battle between the two is inevitable.

NANDA:
(*Correspondent*) Yes, it certainly looks like that at the moment. This dispute has been growing for some time. The rains in this area have been so poor this year. Because of this, the river Rohini is too low to water the fields of both the Sakyas and the Koliyas.

MADRI: And there is deadlock over who should have what little water there is. Nanda, if it comes to a battle, which of the two armies do you think is the stronger?

NANDA: Well, there is no doubt that the Sakyas are a tough people, but the Koliyas are better armed . . .

MADRI: I'm going to interrupt you because an enormous commotion has just broken out in both armies. You can see on our pictures now what has caused such a stir. That famous holy man, Gautama the Buddha, just walked between the two armies and has seated himself on the river bank.

NANDA: If he stays there and a battle does break out, he will be directly in the line of fire.

MADRI: Extraordinary! He's just sitting there cross-legged, perfectly still. He looks as if nothing in the world could worry him.

NANDA: He's certainly having an effect. Marada, one of the great Lords of the Sakyas, and his commanders-in-chief are riding towards the Buddha and Vasu, Lord of the Koliyas, is also now preparing to talk to the Buddha. We will be moving closer to hear what is being said.

(*A meeting takes place between the Buddha, the Lord of the Sakyas and the Lord of the Koliyas.*)

MARADA: Look! It's not our fault. It's those fools of Koliyas . . .

VASU: What are you talking about? You're stealing our water!

THE BUDDHA: Noble Lords, do not speak harsh words. What do such words achieve? They make hatred grow both in others and within ourselves. Once spoken they poison our inner peace.

(*The two men look ashamed.*)

MARADA: All right, but if we can't water our lands, many of my people will die.

THE BUDDHA: Great Lord, if you go to battle, is it not certain that many of your people will be slain?

MARADA: Yes of course.

THE BUDDHA: Do you not both want your people to be happy? Listen to me. The person who hurts others for the sake of happiness will never find happiness themselves. Gentlemen, life is priceless. Do not stake what is priceless against a few fields and a stretch of water. For the sake of life and the happiness of your people you must share the water this year.

VASU: Our water is very low . . .

MARADA: "*Our* water!" It's not yours—it's *ours*!

THE BUDDHA: "Our", "mine"—what do these words mean? When your people are dead on the field of battle, what then do they possess? The water is here and it will give life to all of you if you will only help each other. Do not let your pride defeat you. Are you going to let people die because you two are so full of pride that you cannot agree?

(*The Buddha talks for a long time to the two Lords. He convinces them that they should not fight.*)

MADRI: Lord Marada and Lord Vasu, can you tell us what has been happening this morning? Do you think that there will be a battle?

MARADA: No, there will be no battle. This morning my heart was full of anger and hate but the Buddha's words have made me see that such feelings are foolish.

VASU: We have both learnt a great deal this morning. Now we shall work together for our people. We shall share the water. The Buddha's wisdom has saved us from war.

What have you remembered?

1. The Buddha taught that people should try to become

2. The Buddha was against the killing of

3. The Buddha allowed men and women to join the

4. The Buddha allowed into the Sangha

5. The Buddha encouraged his followers to become filled with

6. The Buddha said that the belief in a separate self was an

S	l	a	u	g	h	t	e	r		
A										
S										
O										
C										
I										

7. Complete the word puzzle.

Clues across
1. He tried to kill the Buddha.
3. Between the Koliyas and the Sakyas the Buddha prevented a

   _ _ _ _ _ _.
5. Buddhists believe that most people have too much of this.
7. We use this word to claim ownership.

Clues down
1. The Buddha faced this to save the life of others.
2. Do possessions matter when you are this?
4. When you achieved Enlightenment you would not feel this again.
6. Not 'I' but another word for the self.

What do you know?

8. Why did some of the religious priests dislike the Buddha?

9. Complete the following saying of the Buddha:
    'The person who for the sake of their own happiness hurts others

    — — — — — — — — — — — — — — — — — — — — —

    — — — — — — — — —.'

10. Explain what the Buddha did to prevent a war between the people of Koliyas and the people of Sakyas.

11. Write a short story for which the following passage from the Dhammapada would be a suitable title.
    'Forsake anger, give up pride.' (The Dhammapada, 17:221)

What do you think?

12. Many Buddhists are pacifists. What does a pacifist believe?

13. What do you think of the pacifists' attitude to war?

14. What do you think are the signs of being too much concerned with yourself? Do you think too much about yourself?

15. Read carefully through 'The Parable of Me and Mine', the story of Sarida and Nina on pages. What do you think this story is telling us?

16. Can you think of a time when you had an argument like the one Sarida and Nina had? If so, describe what happened.

For forty-five years the Buddha helped people to find Nirvana for themselves. However, when he was about eighty years old he fell ill. He knew that death was not far away.

A few months later, with his closest friends gathered around him, the Buddha died. Even when he knew he was going to die he remained totally calm and content. He continued to teach right up to the end. "Seek salvation in the truth alone," he told his followers. "Rely on yourself, and do not rely on the help of anyone else." With his last breath he reminded his followers that each person had to free themselves from hate and desire and that no one could do this for them. "Work out your salvation with effort" were his final words. Then the Buddha entered into a deep meditation. So it was, in death as in life, with no fuss or disturbance, he gently died.

'The glorious chariots of kings wear out, and the body wears out and grows old; but the virtue of the good never grows old, and thus they can teach good to those who are good.'
(The Dhammapada, 11:151)

Today Buddhists are to be found all over the world, including Britain. The beliefs and practices of Buddhists vary widely. Some Buddhists continue to wear a yellow robe and live as the first followers of the Buddha did. They follow the rules of the Sangha very strictly. Some Buddhists wear ordinary clothes and work in offices or factories.

These differences have not happened recently or come about simply because Buddhism has become more popular in countries like Britain, America, France and Germany. The leader of an eight-hundred-year-old Japanese School of Buddhism once wrote that it is not at all necessary to withdraw from the world in order to become a perfect Buddhist. Their founder, the Shonin Shinran, was married and lived as the world does. Such Buddhists believe that they need not mark themselves as different from other people by what they wear or what they do.

These views were never rejected by other Buddhists. After all, when the Buddha was alive he had encouraged people to find their own path to Nirvana. Following the teaching of the Buddha himself, Buddhists accepted that truth could take many different forms. As one famous English Buddhist, Christmas Humphreys, wrote, 'The range of Buddhism. . . is enormous, and within its vast and tolerant field all manner of human thought is welcome, and every method of treading the Way has its honourable place.'

Christmas Humphreys (centre), a British Buddhist.
Christmas Humphreys was the founder of The Buddhist Society.
This society is the oldest Buddhist organisation in Europe.

The huge Buddha at Kamukura in Japan. As with many statues of the Buddha this statue is not meant to look like Gautama Buddha. The statue represents the Tathagata, the spiritual principle within Gautama Buddha and all of the Buddhas before him.

As we might expect, Buddhist beliefs about Gautama the Buddha vary a great deal. All Buddhists accept that he was a man who achieved Enlightenment of the mind. However, many Buddhists would want to say much more.

For many Buddhists, although Gautama is deeply respected, the details of his life are not important. These Buddhists believe that there have been many Buddhas before Gautama. All of them had within them the same spiritual principle called the *Tathagata*. For many Buddhists the teaching of Gautama Buddha is not therefore the teaching of one wise man. He is just one among many Buddhas who show us the spiritual principle of the Tathagata.

Some Buddhists believe that simply showing love and devotion towards the spiritual principle, the Tathagata, can help them to achieve Enlightenment. Such Buddhists praise and worship the Buddha daily. For them the Buddha is like a God with unlimited power and unlimited compassion. It is a living spirit of love and devotion.

For some Buddhists the life of Gautama the Buddha as a human person is very important. The Buddha reminds them that any person who seeks perfect joy can achieve Enlightenment. He showed people that with will and determination, anger and greed can be controlled. He is proof that all of us are capable of being a Buddha.

Buddhism appeals to all sorts of people from all walks of life. Buddhism is not just for highly intelligent or very clever people. At the heart of what the Buddha was saying there is a message of peace, joy and contentment which can be understood by everyone.

A soldier went on a long journey to speak to a follower of the Buddha. The soldier asked, "What is the message of the Buddha?" The follower answered, "Do not what is evil. Do what is good. Keep your mind pure. This is the teaching of the Buddha".

"Is that all?" said the soldier. "Every child of five knows this."

"Maybe so," the follower replied, "but few people of eighty can practise it."